healing for no one but me

by jennae cecelia

jennae cecelia

healing for no one but me

healing for no one but me

in a time when the years have felt
heavy and uncertain,
healing for no one but me is meant to
make you feel powerful and less alone in your
thoughts, while also touching on the realities
that happen in day-to-day life. whether you
have anxiety, depression, lost someone you
love, went through a breakup, have hit a
rough patch, or many rough patches, this
book is a healing process. but remember it is
your healing process.

i hope you find comfort here.

love,
jennae

healing for no one but me

you do not even know
how much the story
you are scared to tell
could help someone else
out of their own
isolated hell.

repeat after me;
i am worthy of being here today
exactly as i want to be.
i do not need to change
or mold myself
just to make other people
comfortable with me.

i do not allow people
to get close to me.
and i do not allow myself
to get close to them.
a happy medium.
i stay somewhere in the middle
of friend, but not close enough
to be in my wedding.
i will call you sometimes,
but you will not be hearing from me
in an emergency at 3 AM.
i do not allow myself to be any more
than in the middle because losing people
does not hurt as bad
if you do not fully let them in.

i will say
i am going to be confident today,
then my messy bun
falls out of place.
and my cozy outfit screams
i rolled out of bed.
and my makeup-less face
makes me look half-dead.
but maybe these thoughts
spinning in my head
are not seen by others
because they are too busy thinking
of their "flaws" instead.

that is the thing about
picking yourself up
out of your own personal hell.
no one sees how hard it is
except you.
all they see is that you,
"finally got your shit together."

today someone honked at me as i drove
a little too slow for their liking.
and all i could think was,
if only they knew
all that i was going through right now
maybe they would have been
a little more patient.
today someone tapped their foot loudly
behind me in line at the store.
impatient with my shaky hands
fumbling to find my credit card.
and all i could think was,
if only they knew
all that i was going through right now
maybe they would have been
a little more patient.
but they did not know.
we do not know.
we just make our own assumptions.
when really there are paths of pain
people are walking
and we never even see a glimpse,
because we are too worried
about where we are going next
and not *where they stand right now.*

lately it feels like,
"i am so sorry."
"i am thinking of you."
"i hope you are safe and alright."
are the only words that i write.
there is a heaviness
with each message and call.
and i am constantly wondering
when i will get through this all.
i find myself crawling into spaces
that feel safe,
and shutting out the world.
but then feeling guilty for thinking
i can just turn it all off and push it away.
i do not know what tomorrow holds,
but i am taking it day by day.
and i think that is more than ok.

i am trying to do more tangible things.
make with my hands.
create with color.
dust a book off my shelves.
i want to feel more alive here
and less like i am just simply existing
in worlds that are not even mine.
it is easy to get stuck in a pit,
but when i finally look up
i feel guilty for having nothing to show for it.

this circle i have drawn around myself
is filled with comfort
and moving beyond the line is not easy.
but how will i ever get anywhere new
if i do not expand my circle?

i am healing here.
between the silence
and the breeze.
tending to wounds
i have been afraid to see.
healing for no one but me.

people have their seasons.
some are long.
some are just for a brief moment in time.
some end unexpectedly.
some are reborn when they are just right.
trust that the people
who are in your life
are meant to be by your side
for however long that may be.

dear me now,

i know you are afraid
that life will not go
how you planned for it to be.
that dreams you have
will not be reached.
that you will not
move beyond the soil
you have always found comfort in.
but i am here to tell you
that all the things
you have played out in your mind,
wished for one thousand times,
are working out
just as you always knew they would
when you let go and trusted in timing.

love,
me next year

there is only so much healing
i can do in this space
that does not allow
healing at my own pace,
and only,
"hurry up and just be ok."

if nothing is forever,
why does this pain never leave?
why can i not move past
something that is long gone?
why can i not find relief?

i want to come out of this
as someone that i do not recognize.
finally taking off this disguise.
because i am no longer afraid
of being my true self
for not only me
but everyone else.

just think,
one day the puzzle pieces
will fall into place
and everything will make sense
and be ok.
and then when life comes
and knocks you down.
and it will.
you will feel pressured to scramble
and put the pieces back together
and move past the aftermath
that came along with it.
but picking yourself up
and putting things back together
does not have to be
calculated or rushed.
you have done it once before,
so you know it will come.

there are seeds in this soil
i am waiting to see bloom.
but i am forgiving
and patient now,
because i know how it feels
to be rushed into something
too soon.

the past is long gone,
but sometimes it is
a whisper in the wind
reminding me that it helped me
be who i am today.
the good and the bad.
the ugly and afraid.
the past is not here to haunt
it is here to remind me
that i made it through the times
i thought i never would escape.
here i am with a future brand new.

it is ok to be in the dark.
in the unknown.
in the messy in-between.
there is so much good
that comes from working on yourself
in a place that lacks full clarity.

i have so much growth to be made
but i am taking it day by day.
not rushing where i need to be
in order to make my healing journey
comfortable for anyone but me.

do you ever have those days
where your hands are too chapped
but no lotion will help
and the itchiness makes you
want to scream?
those days where your
leggings do not feel as cozy as they should
and instead, they feel like an entrapment
sticking to your leg hairs
you still need to shave?
those days where your hair
is too greasy but also too dry
and the low bun you put it in
does not look as effortless as everyone else
makes it seem?
do you ever have those days
where you feel like you are a stranger
in your own skin?
yeah, me too.

i think people tell you
that healing is from beginning until end
and then your problem just goes away.
but i have found
that healing is a journey
with many detours and unexpected turns.
and just when you think you are ok,
and just when you think you have
resolved the issue,
that is when the journey starts over again.
healing is a journey
with multiple different ends.

healing deep wounds
is not a matter of time and forgetfulness.
it is accepting that those wounds
have shaped the story you now carry.
and oh what a beautiful story
you have turned this pain into.

and i will keep saying
almost.
maybe.
tomorrow.
i would love to be there one day.
i will press forward in life
thinking tomorrow is still so far away.
but when i meet tomorrow for breakfast
and realize yesterday's tomorrow is now today.
i wonder how many tomorrows
i will meet and keep saying
i will go for my dream the next day.

today i woke up to the sun saying hi
and somehow that was all the comfort
i needed to feel just fine.
but only fine for a short time
because as i started my day
and looked at my phone with no notifications-
that made me feel even more far away.
the toast i made was burnt
from my wandering mind
and the coffee i poured
spilled down the sides.
i could not find socks that matched
and my only clean sweater
had a stain that was hard to hide.
i could have put it away
and taken from the plethora
of clothes hanging up,
but none of them felt right.
i drove with my wipers on full blast
because the rain had now
taken the suns place.
and i looked at myself in the rearview mirror
and silently said to myself,
how did i get to here?

i hope today is your day.
the sun hits your face just right.
your favorite t-shirt fits the way you like.
your hair is what
you have always tried to achieve.
there is no line in the drive-thru
to get your coffee.
your skin feels dewy.
and someone sends you a message
that makes you smile.
i hope today you feel the most right
you have in a while.

they may be
walking down the aisle.
they may be
welcoming tiny new feet into their home.
they may be
making big purchases.
they may be
anything but alone.
they may seem
like they have their life fully together.
they may seem
like their list is full of check marks.
but do not feel like you have to
accomplish everything from a list
that does not even fit what you want.
do not feel like you have to answer
the "when are you going to do it?" remarks.

i am constantly reminded
that life is full of both good
and bad surprises.
like finding money in your pocket
you did not know was there.
while simultaneously
finding your car with a flat tire.
i am constantly reminded
that life is a balancing act.
you cannot only have the good
without getting some bad back.

i keep telling myself one day
i will be that woman
i have always envisioned being.
the one who does not
have a worry about who she is
or where she is going.
the one that does not avoid photos
because it is evidence
that she is a stranger to herself.
the one who does not avoid mirrors
but rather, smiles at her reflection.
the one who does not wait
until the last minute to pay a bill
or fill her refrigerator with food.
who is that woman anyways?
someone i am slowly meeting day by day.
she is getting there
but it is ok to not be perfect.
it is ok to make slow changes
while also not changing at all.

i like dandelions better than roses.
and barefoot walking
more than wearing nice shoes.
and you told me
i am so simple and easy to please.
that i can grow from any situation with ease.
but really i have just learned
i have to be adaptable
to all that is around me.

my favorite color was always blue
if you asked me.
not because i liked it,
but it seemed like a simple answer
that no one would question.
my favorite color was always orange
if you really knew me.
and depending how close you were to me
i was either your friend
whose favorite color was blue,
or your friend
whose favorite color was orange.
and no one knew
that was how i kept people in categories
of close or far enough away.

you are like butter.
you soften yourself
for those who you feel you can be soft with
or you are hard as a rock
and not easy to work with.
and then once in a while,
really only once-
you will meet someone
who gets the melted butter version of you
and that is when you know they are the one.

today has the chance
to be a beautiful fresh start.
put on a new pair of sheets.
wipe the counters clean.
today is your new beginning.
a chance to reset yourself
for a tomorrow you will not dread.

i take brief moments.
sit and enjoy the stars
and the way the grass
moves in the wind.
because those are present moments
and i need to exist there more.

i did not fall in love with you
because years went on
and it felt more comfortable
to stay than leave.
because we both know
i am quick to start over
if i am not happy.
i fell in love with you
because home took the place of alone
and i did not feel scared to let you in.
no more knocking at the door
because you knew you were welcome.

i still do not really know
if i am quiet or loud.
or if i am lost or found.
i do not know if i like tea
or if it is only coffee for me.
i still do not really know
who i am.
the world makes me think
that who i am needs to change.
because who i am does not match
what i see on my social media page.

a lot has changed since we last met.
i like spicy food and black coffee
and i never thought
that would be something i would admit.
i do not wear as much makeup
to hide what never needed
to be hidden.
and do not run just to be thin.
the tears hidden behind my eyes
fall when they need to.
and i do not say i am ok if am not.
i let my emotions come through.
i got a degree in a subject
you said i was terrible at.
but communication was really
something that *you* lacked.
a lot has changed since we last met.
you would not even recognize me now.
and i am so proud of that.

they say your rainbow will come
and things will be ok,
but you still cannot help
but wonder what would have
come before the rain.

i am the woman with no calendar.
no plans written in ink.
my life can be quite messy.
there are dishes filled high in the sink.
i am the woman in a hurry.
hair thrown upon my head.
my gas tank on nearly empty.
i forgot to make my bed.
but i am also the woman
that sees art everywhere she goes.
my pen always ready to write a story.
i will remember the details about you
that no one else knows.
that is more important, for me.

i do not want to wait for another life
to not care what people think of me.
i want to run free in the wildflowers.
say hi to strangers i do not know.
i want to invite people over for dinner
and not care if they do not show.
i want to wear no makeup
and not feel like i have to explain
my lack of being put together.
i want to eat burgers and pizza
and not say that was the first thing i ate all day.
i do not want to wait for another life
to not care about the ideas people have of me.
i want to be in the here and now feeling free.

to my future son or daughter.
if you are reading this one day.
i hope you never
feel compelled to be anyone
but who you truly feel you are.
that you are not afraid
of the next day to come.
that if hurt happens
you are not ashamed of those scars.
i hope you know how needed you are.

my hands may never feel the same.
today they closed a chapter
that caused so much pain.
they waved goodbye to a story
they thought would never end.
here begins a journey
of never having
to beg to be read again.

i drink my coffee when i know
it is still way too hot
and act surprised when it burns me.
but i am so trusting
that maybe this time it will not
when it is obvious there is no other ending.

i think it is ok
to be a little bit selfish.
you do not have to share
your hopes and dreams.
you do not have to share
where you plan to go
or what you want to see.
it is ok to trust your gut
and protect your heart.
it is ok to be a little selfish.
it is *your* life.
do not forget that part.

nothing is the same as what it once was.
and while that is scary it is also beautiful.
here i am with the fresh start
i always wanted.
and yes i do not know
where i am going or what is to come.
but *i will* get there one way or another.

i am in the wildflower fields
searching for peace in the petals
and strength in the wind.
i know it is coming for me.
i know i deserve it.

she has a pinterest board
with quotes saved about
doing crunches or sit ups to earn cupcakes.
and i have quotes saved too,
but they are all about being
deep in my feelings
while eating comfort food.

-we could not be more different

i am not the same person
i was last year
or the year before.
and while that might seem scary,
because people stop recognizing me
for who i once was;
i remember that
who i am changing into now
is someone i always dreamed of.

some people can not handle
the positive growth you are making.
because it requires them
to leave a comfort zone
they have had with you for so long.
it requires them realizing
that you are no longer
who you used to be
and they do not really have anything
in common with you now
except past memories.

maybe right now
you are not supposed to be at this destination
that feels so right but also so wrong.
and feels so comfortable
but you are also wondering
where leaving would take you.
just the thought makes your stomach flutter
with excitement and nervousness all at once.
do you want to be where you are right now
next year,
or even in just a few months?

you go ahead and take up the space.
you go ahead and dance in the rain.
you go ahead and talk as loud as you want.
you go ahead and share your dreams.
you go ahead and run down the empty streets.
you deserve to be seen here.
you do not need to hide,
or be quiet,
or keep your dreams to yourself.
unless you want to- that is different.
but do not be afraid of owning your life here.
you are just as important as everyone else.

i am so glad that we did not work out.
i thought for so long
that breathing different air
and seeing different places
would kill me slowly.
and for some time it did.
but the longer we breathed separately
and did things without the other.
i realized you were really suffocating me
from all there was to discover.

to the girl i was back then,
i am sorry i made you feel
like you did not matter.
that you were not beautiful.
that you did not have
the ability to chase your dreams.
i am sorry i tore you down
any chance i could get.
i am sorry that you never felt seen.
you deserved so much better than me
constantly dressing you in insults.
i hope you can forgive me now.
we have come so far since then.
i can not wait for you to see how.

you told me i was broken.
that it should not be this hard to be happy.
why was i always sad?
why was i always sleeping?
you said i was broken,
but really you were breaking me
while simultaneously telling me
i was overreacting.

it is ok.
i am so much better now.
and i did not need you to do it.
i did it on my own somehow.
i pulled myself up.
i started getting dressed.
i went on walks.
i treated my mind
to the right kind of rest.
it is ok.
i am so much better now.
not that you probably care,
but i do.
because you used to tell me
i could never do better without you.

there is this woman i have in my head
that is so much better than the me today.
a woman i have been trying to meet.
a woman who knows more,
is more,
has more.
a woman that seems so far out of reach.
but i am slowly realizing that woman is me
screaming out the pieces of myself
that i find so hard to see.

take a moment today
to meet the sun-kissed morning for coffee,
before the world awakens
and the silence is shaken.
breathe in the infinite possibilities
of a fresh canvas day.

how freeing to remember today
that this life can be walked
in any way.
do not forget
who the author of your story is
when you feel like you have no say.

this year may bring you
eagerness to move
quickly and efficiently,
but there is beauty on the walk
of patience and imperfection.

people like me should not
wear white shirts.
the type that leave the lid off
the boiling pot,
because it is one less dish to clean.
the type to wipe up a few drops
of spilt coffee with their sock,
because there is not enough time
to do it properly.
the type to have an electric toothbrush
that has not been charged in weeks,
because somehow that is too daunting.
people like me should not
wear white shirts,
because there is no way to hide
what we do not want others to see.

and as for today?
maybe this is not
where you pictured yourself.
maybe you think
you are so far from where you want to go.
just know that life is always a journey,
even when you get to your goal.

i was searching for comfort
in the most rigid of places
and wondering why
i could not seem to fit in.
but i am meant to follow the breeze
and live without strings.
letting go of limitations
is where it begins.

my favorite pair of jeans
do not fit like they used to
and typically that would bother me.
but now i am more concerned
with forcing a smile
that does not fit me.

anytime something bad happened
in an oufit i wore,
i would give it away.
i had to.
the memories attached to those items
were way too hard to think about,
let alone wear.
i could feel the anxiety and sadness
hanging onto their threads.
needless to say there were many seasons
where my closet was empty and so was i.

i am learning
how to love my life
for its seasons.
not wish for my seasons
to change faster
or before it is time.

it starts with the simple tasks
becoming hard.
like leaving texts on read.
abandoning emails.
not paying bills i know are due.
the anxiety starts to take over
and makes even the simplest of tasks
feel impossible to do.

you have sunrises to catch
and dreams to achieve.
you have a purpose here.
you matter to me.

welcome to another friday
you waited all week for.
a weekend you thought about
as you typed on your computer
long past 8 PM.
and as you sat in meetings
where you were physically present,
but where was your head?
come sunday you will have
the "sunday scaries"
about what monday has in store.
so when will the weekends
become what you live in
instead of live for?

happiness peaking out
like the sun on the horizon.
that is just the sign i need
to keep going.
keep moving.
keep growing.
keep having belief.

as your life becomes heavy to hold,
maybe they look like
they are on top of the world
from your view.
but in reality their world
is crumbling beneath their feet,
while they look back at you
and think you have it altogether too.

what does not make sense now
will be screaming with certainty
in the future.

it is much more fulfilling
to create something brand new,
than copy and paste what others do.

you can ask everyone for advice,
but at the end of the day
only you know
what is best for your life.
only you know
what direction is right.

second chances exist,
but i stopped handing them out
to the people who kept coming back
for the third,
fourth,
and fifth time.
and still expected me
to welcome them with warm arms
and an open mind.

you may have a past
that is daunting to think about,
but here you are with a future
that is glowing.

the past can only come back
in my mind.
kind of like you.

maybe your light and hopeful morning
has turned into a heavy day.
a slow morning rise
now a fast paced race.
but as you close your eyes
at the end of the day.
breathe in the here and now.
it will be ok.

today you may feel hope
in the untouched tomorrow.
with promises you
have plans to meet up with.
as optimisim runs
through your mind.
tonight let us cheers
to confidence about life.

you told me that i wore
such a beautiful smile.
little did you know
i was putting on an outfit
that had not fit me in awhile.
one that was a little uncomfortable
and had to be forced on each day.
the color was not even close
to my favorite shade.
but i kept wearing that smile
because everyone told me
how beautiful it made me.

not everyone is going
to be able to see your vision.
we do not all see the world
through eyes with the same prescription.
it is ok to be the only one rooting
for your decision.

i say i want the loud street noises,
chatter down the sidewalks,
and access to quicky get
my favorite iced coffee.
but i also want the slow life
on acreage with berry bushes,
apple trees,
and no close access-
making for intentional ventures only.
i say i want to stay off the internet
and social media.
be unknown to the world.
but i also want to share my words
and hear the stories of others
i may never get the chance
to physically meet.
but maybe what my mind and body
are telling me is that i need
a balance of these things.
to honor the moments
i want to be alone
and also when i want to be loud and seen.
to be more intentional
but also be open to what adventure brings.

there are summertime books
about falling in love with someone unexpected.
at the beach in a small town with no one around,
but somehow there is someone just for you.
and these stories make you feel like
you will have moments like that too.
except the beaches are quiet here
and everyone is in a rush.
how come the books made it sound like
it is that easy to fall in love?

healing for me
is going away to places
people can not find me.
somewhere i can escape.
healing for me does not involve a team
it is my own to face.
because healing is an individual race.
you can run, walk, stop, or jog
whenever you want along the way.
but go at *your* pace
and do not worry if you stray.

i have come to terms with the fact
that i do not get to know
what your favorite tv show is anymore.
or what you order
at your new favorite restaurant.
or if you still do not like
to go on evening walks.
do you still hate the mornings
that i love so much?
do you still leave the house
in a messy rush?
i have come to terms with the fact
that i do not get to know
all these new versions of you–
if there are any at all.
because maybe you are still refusing
to grow beyond *your* four walls.

there is so much more to me now
than you will ever find out
on my social media page.
sorry it is hard to know the nitty gritty
details about me if you are lurking.
i no longer feel the need to share
every detail online.
i can make breakfast
without posting a picture.
get coffee with a friend
and just enjoy the moment together.
see a bright full moon
or a beautiful sunrise
and not reach for my phone-
just look at the sky.
there is so much more to me now
than you will ever find out
on my social media page.
i no longer feel the need to show up
with every detail of me
in hopes you would see it
and feel like you were missing
out on so much.

someone asked about you
today at the grocery store
not realizing you had been
gone long before.
i answered in a whisper
and they looked at me
with pity in their eyes.
i hated that.
i hated that.
do not make me feel even less than alright.
i do not know what to say
when people ask about you.
so sometimes it is just easier to pretend
what they think too-
that you are still here and nothing has changed.
but it is so obvious you are not in this place.

i used to care too much
about what people think.
but now i do not mind
having people come over
with dishes in the kitchen sink.
i do not try to impress people
just so i do not have to worry
what they are judging me for.
life is much easier when i do not care
if there are a few crumbs on the floor.

if you knew me before five years ago
and not anymore,
you do not really know the me now.
you have met me.
you have interacted with me.
but only a me that is just a ghost
to the me today.
who you think you know
is so far away.

i finally realized that
i did not deserve to be told
my ideas were silly,
or that i should not like
ranch with my pizza,
or that my hair should only
be worn down
even though
i liked it up just as much.
i finally realized that
what you made a big deal about
were always the small things.
nit-picking so i could never
be doing anything right.
i deserve the small things.
i deserve simple happiness.
i finally realized that with you
everything was a fight.

i was good at being alone.
i was good at getting lost in my mind.
i was good at finding comfort in myself.
that was what i did all this time.
so when one day i had
more than just me to share
"me" things with,
i did not know how much
i really needed it.

i never really liked vanilla cake,
or going to church on sunday,
or watching the news.
but somehow i thought
that would get me closer to you.
so every birthday
i ate the cake unamused.
and every sunday sat feeling guilty
in the church pew.
and never once did you thank me
for giving up so much me
to please you.

i am ok with the fact
that the girl from my past
brought me pain and ache.
i am not mad at her.
i am grateful she carried me here.
there is nothing i would change.
the story we wrote together is one
i will never try to hide
or erase off the page.

you have so many days left here.
so many to see through.
so many to get to.
so many to enjoy.
so many to hate.
but those days are all stories
to tell one day.

the day will come when you
stop typing in their name
at the top of your social media page.
the day will come when you
stop trying to find out
as much as you can about them.
regretting unfriending them at 3 AM.
the day will come when you
no longer care who they are seeing,
where they are going,
or if they cut their hair.
and maybe right now that seems
so hard to believe,
but one day when you go to type their name
they will not even be in your search history.

i love that now instead of asking
my favorite color
you ask me what i have for dreams.
and instead of calling me crazy,
you chase them with me.

you do not need to suffer alone
in your room
with the music blaring.
and your notebook filled.
and your favorite show on for distraction.
there is beauty in help.
there is beauty in asking.

i have made peace with myself.
it happened last year.
i told her i was sorry.
and she said it back.
i told her i should have
been more forgiving of
what i thought she lacked.
she told me she should have
thought of me instead of only
who she was then.
she said she was sorry for making
my accomplishments hard to get.
but i said,
"do not do that.
do not make yourself
feel like you did not do enough.
mental health is a journey
and can make life rough."

what is the rush?
why hurry through life?
fill agendas quickly
that do not even feel right.
what is the rush?
there is so much
to stop and see along the way.
who cares if you do not
check off the list in the same order,
or in the same time frame?

i have gone down roads that no one knows
and got so lost i could not see.
and all that time people thought
i was just fine and even now
would be surprised to find out
all i was keeping inside me.

you deserve to be loved
for who you are
and what you believe.
you deserve to be loved
even if you think you are
hard to fully reach.
you deserve to be loved
like you love
but have yet to receive.

and if you showed up
knocking at your own door
looking on at the person
you were once before,
would you close it
or welcome yourself in?
maybe this is your chance to give
yourself the forgivenss you never did get.

i thought if i packed my bags
and moved myself somewhere new,
i could start over as a person
who was a stranger to even myself.
but as i started upacking my bags,
and placing knick knacks on the shelves,
pieces of the old me started to unpack too.
even when i tried so hard
to pretend i was brand new.
slowly my blinds closed again
and and i did not wave
at any of my new "friends."
and now i was left with the fact
that i could not just pick myself up
and start over without addressing
what was going on beyond just
wanting a do-over.

there are places with green grass,
waterfalls and sunrises
that i have always wanted to see.
and they feel so far out of reach.
but as i sit here today
and breathe in the sunny morning
with my hand around my mug,
and the other placed against my heart.
being present
and enjoying where i am here
is a very good start.

take a deep breath with me,
let it out,
and repeat;
today i will not apologize
for my beautiful mind
and my body that carries me
through this life.
i am beautifully alive here.
i am so important and so wanted.
i will not let that be forgotten.

the healing you are doing
may seem so small,
but the process of healing
is just starting at all.
i am proud you made it here.
do not worry if you have setbacks.
that is the beautful thing,
this is not your last chance.

hold onto the feeling you have today.
chapter one.
the excitement and wonder
for all that is to come.
so as time goes on
and trials come and go.
you remember why you started,
why you should never give up,
and why you are more than enough
to make your ideas grow.

jennae cecelia

to read more work by jennae cecelia,
check out her other nine books:

the sun will rise and so will we

the moon will shine for us too

losing myself brought me here

dear me at fifteen

i am more than my nightmares

uncaged wallflower- extended edition

i am more than a daydream

uncaged wallflower

bright minds empty souls

jennae cecelia

about the author

www.JennaeCecelia.com

@JennaeCecelia on Instagram

@JennaeCecelia on TikTok

jennae cecelia is a best-selling author
of inspirational poetry books
and is best known for her books,
the sun will rise and so will we
and *uncaged wallflower.*

she is also an inspirational speaker
who digs into topics like
self-love, self-care, mental health,
and body positivity.

her mission is to encourage people
to reach their full potential and
live a life filled with positivity and love.

jennae cecelia